WE MAKE A
COMMUNITY GARDEN

TAKING CIVIC ACTION

Tana Hensley

CiViCS

FOR THE **REAL** WORLD™

Rosen
Classroom™

There is an empty lot
on my street. We make
a community garden.

We dig the dirt with small
shovels. We plant seeds
in the garden.

The plants need to be watered
every day. A watering can
does the job!

We grow vegetables
in our garden. There are
so many carrots!

We spend time together
in the garden. It brings
our community together.

Our garden makes the community better.
Everyone enjoys the garden!

WORDS TO KNOW

carrots

shovel

watering
can